LIGHTIN' UP

A rousing collection
of flame-boyant cartoons
by
Roy Schlemme

AuthorHouse™
1663 Liberty Drive
Bloomington, IN 47403
www.authorhouse.com
Phone: 1-800-839-8640

First published by AuthorHouse   2/17/2011

ISBN: 978-1-4567-3457-2 (sc)

Library of Congress Control Number: 2011901661

Printed in the United States of America

*Any people depicted in stock imagery provided by Thinkstock are models,
and such images are being used for illustrative purposes only.
Certain stock imagery © Thinkstock.*

This book is printed on acid-free paper.

For John and Hilary.
(The fantabulous Finnises of Faversham)

R. SCHLEMME

More fun than a two-horned rhino!

But that's only the humble opinion of the artiste who assembled this collection of disjointed scribblings aimed at only the most highly intelligent and humor oriented of audiences. Hopefully, your three-and-a-half-minute excursion through *Lightin' Up* will not only whet your appetite for more, but provoke many questions as well, not the least of which would be "What the hell was that all about?".

— *Roy Schlemme*

"It's another spectacular sunset, Kimmy.
You'll really enjoy them in a few years when you're taller."

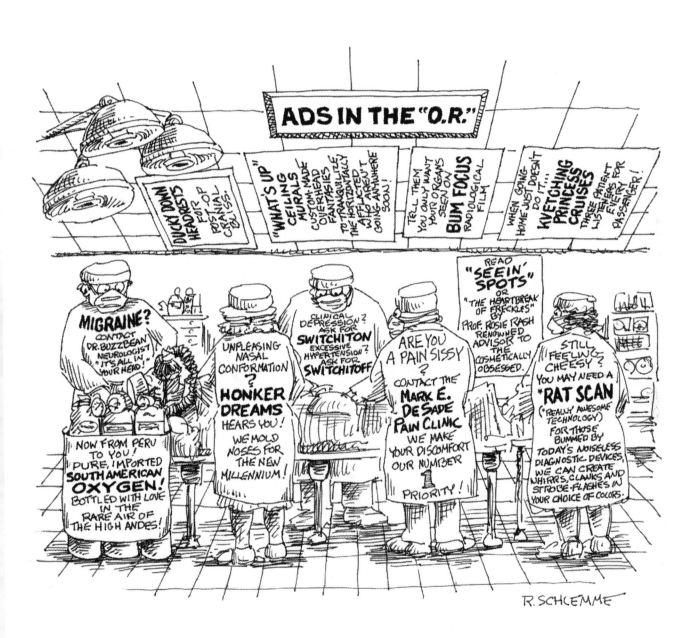

"Since Captain Dennis plans on using
his beta waves to guide today's flight,
we're requesting all passengers to turn off
their brains until further notice."

"Finally, something worth leaving behind for the kids."

Ancient English ruins.

"The Admiralty rates him
a fair captain, albeit a harsh one."

R. SCHLEMME

Joggers' Hell.

"20% of your first place money or a double hernia!"

"We can wait, Arthur!"

"Please don't say anything. Dancers are
skittish enough to begin with."

THE GHOST OF CHRISTMAS TRASH

"Rephrase our house listing to read
*'Moving, spectacular view,
halfway down rugged hillside'*!"

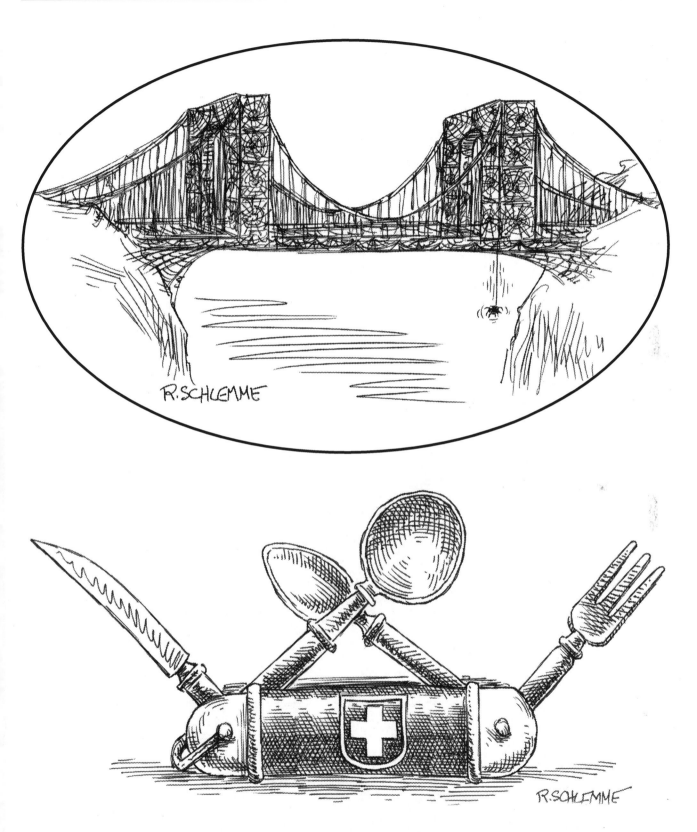

Swiss Army knife, spoon, fork and soup ladle.

"I always said that teaching it *'fetch'* was the easy part."

R.SCHLEMME

"Bless this ship and all those who
take tax write-offs on her."

"The hell with saving the condor!
Save the ornithologist!"

"It squeaks whenever I throw a royal tantrum."

"Try to hit the ball harder, sweetie. Pretend it's
the severed head of a certain deadbeat dad
who regularly misses child support payments."

"Sorry, I just don't see a revue like
'Crustaceans on Parade' as having
much potential, in spite of featuring
post-performance *'Eat the Cast'* parties."

"I must admit results might've turned out a touch better
if my cell phone hadn't rung at that exact moment."

"...and their half-eaten salami on white indicates
a diet dangerously high in sodium and bad cholesterol."

"They just don't write songs like that anymore."

"The plant on my left produces lovely, fragrant,
pink blossoms every spring while the right-hand one
wraps its tendrils around an unsuspecting victim's neck,
then, after choking them to death, drains every
drop of blood from their lifeless body...
or is it just the other way around?"

"My avian sources inform me that
'tweet' can be interpreted 326 different ways."

"It's happened again. We're missing
more mice from the LSD experiments!"

"A nice wash and blowdry or shall I
just feed them a few, small white mice?"

"I often wonder what Michelangelo
might've done with pressed tin."

"Floors, please!"

"So, *'Parsley'*, are we expected to believe that, on
the night your partners, *'Onion'* and *'Mushroom'*, tried to
smother my client, *'T-bone'*, you were only present as a garnish?"

"Under different circumstances, I'd find his hairy bod
and skintight black breeches a major turn-on."

"Then, you'll wonder why they grew up all scrambled."

R. SCHLEMME

"Up it another peg, coach.
I smell a new personal best coming on."

"Little pervert!"

"You don't have anything to read, do you?"

R. SCHLEMME

LITTLE KNOWN IN WESTERN LORE WERE THE MANY INTENSE BATTLES BETWEEN THE JAMES BOYS AND THEIR SMALL OUTLAW BANDS.

"There's something almost poetic in sitting on a hilltop
to watch hundreds of mindless wackos
kick the crap out of each other."

R.SCHLEMME

"Anybody else in here feel a draft?"

R. SCHLEMME

R. SCHLEMME

"Dammit...I asked for decaf!"

"So thinking leaves you with a nasty migrane, too?"

"Care for some fresh argonauts?
They're imported."

THE KING'S **POMPADOUR**

THE MOUSE AND DUCK

THE FUMING DRIVER

CRETIN'S ARMS

THE ANOREXIC'S FEAST

THE COACH AND STEROIDS

THE GRUNGY NIKE

OLD PLASTIC & DEBT

TEN GOLD RINGS

THE **DUKE OF WAYNE**

THE 'YO' MAN

THE HOLLYWOOD ENDING

R. SCHLEMME

"Diagram Five shows it differently."

BEHOLD, AN ENDLESS SEA OF GRASS UPON WHICH THE GREAT SPIRIT HAS PLACED HIS NOBLEST CREATURE – THE MIGHTY BUFFALO!
SUPERB LOCATION FOR A MUNICIPAL PARKING LOT!
R. SCHLEMME

"Nothing says the holidays
like a digital wreath."

"*Doddering old fool! Doddering old fool!*
I've waited over fifty years to say that, Stanley."

"You never bring me worms any more."

"First, there was the *"Missing Dumpty"* report, then sizeable
remnants of eggshell turn up near the village's high wall, and now,
we've just been served the grandest, most tasty breakfast omelet ever.
My conclusions in this case may prove rather unsettling, Watson."

"Pass it along...the game's fixed!"

CAN CARROTS IMPROVE VISION?

"Hey, look...friendly natives! Bet they know
where we might find some stalking lions."

"Are you still able to pick up the late afternoon
sunlight softly defining my cheekbones?"

"Black-capped chickadee...Eastern goldfinch...
Local loony with axe..."

Idiomatic condescension.

In light of his desperate situation,
Leon considers a possible alternative.

"You are growing drowsy...drowzeee...drowzeeee."

R. SCHLEMME

Bad day in le cornfield.

1. MY PERSONAL FEELING IS THAT YOU'RE USING ENTIRELY TOO MUCH YELLOW, MONSIEUR.

2. ARE THOSE CROWS? MY LITTLE NICOLE DRAWS HEAVENLY CROWS! SHALL I BRING HER OUT HERE TO SHOW YOU HER CROWS?

3. HOW MUCH LONGER WILL YOU BE PAINTING, VINCENT? I MUST HARVEST THIS ENTIRE FIELD BEFORE SUNDOWN.

4. I SAY IF A MAN WISHES TO LOP OFF AN EAR FOR NO REASON, THAT'S HIS BUSINESS. SHALL I SPEAK LOUDER?

5. FRAGONARD! INGRES! DELACROIX! THEIR GREAT WORKS ARE THE WELLSPRING FROM WHICH ALL ASPIRING ARTISTS MUST DRAW!

6. ALTHOUGH I RESPECT YOUR UNIQUE WAYS, VAN GOGH, I SIMPLY DON'T SEE HOW YOU'LL BE ABLE TO APPLY PAINT WITH THAT SILLY LITTLE PISTOL.

R. SCHLEMME

"Would it seem overly pushy of me
to take a victory lap here?"

LESS-THAN-EXTREME KICKBOXING FINALS

"...and now, on to tonight's topic:
' Is there life after fruit salad?'."

"It began last month as a small wart on my butt."

"Watch the overwatering!"

"Agreed, they're faster, but no one I know
feels very safe riding a fox."

"It might be nice if you could
maintain our porch light too."

HOW TO KEEP AN
ADJOINING SEAT EMPTY.

R. SCHLEMME

"Paint is not your friend."

"Since we're running so late,
I asked old Wilson to pitch in."

"Mr. Johnson, how many cans was I supposed
to dump into the popcorn machine?"

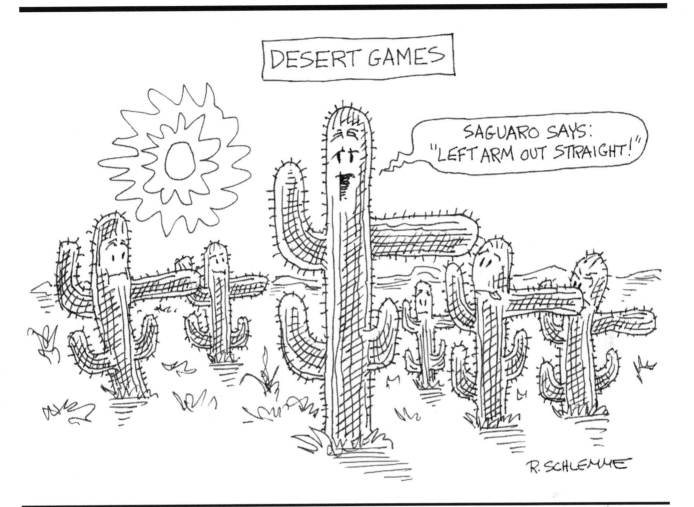

Metal fatigue.
(Due to iron deficiency)

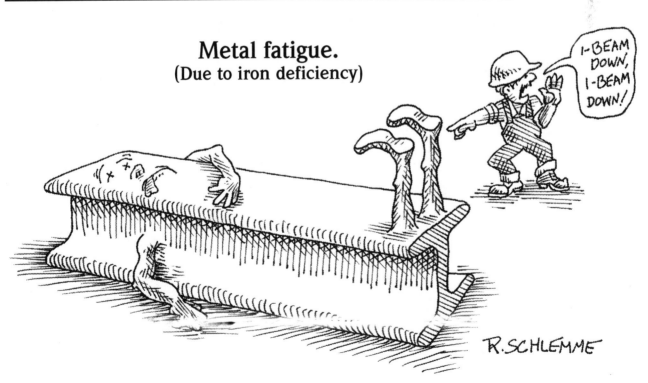

"Give me one good reason why anyone
would choose to immortalize a deadass."

"Mom...Dad...I'm converting to metric!"

"Adding a little sprig of parsley to the same old *'rice and beans'* doesn't really make it a *'vegetable medley'*."

"I somehow remember
pancake breakfasts differently."

"I don't think we're there yet with the *'sibling bonding'* thing."

R.SCHLEMME

Patriot speech.

R. SCHLEMME

"Call me strange, but I love the sound
of whips cracking in the morning."

"Looks like we missed an outstanding
'Voodoo curses and cures' seminar."

R. SCHLEMME

"I've pinpointed that annoying little whine, ma'am...
It's your driver."

"At least the conquistadors
didn't generate any air pollution."

"Now that the siege has weakened them,
we catapult in our ultimate terror weapon...
a hard-charging team of insurance salesmen."

R. SCHLEMME

R. SCHLEMME

Elitist crop dusting.

"Go deep!"

"There's only loaves and fishes, hon.
Want to eat someplace else?"

R. SCHLEMME

"Ever get one of those days when
you don't feel quite all there?"

"I'm finding some communal dining artifacts
of people from the *Early McDonald's period.*"

"Mmm, nothing beats the tantalizing aroma of
freshly debagged breakfast Doritos."

"I'll check, but I feel fairly certain that
we don't stock it in a charcoal gray."

"Looks like a small brush fire!"

"Mind these steps! They're a little uneven!"

R.SCHLEMME

"Follow the swiftly flowing Anatapooka until you reach
a mighty rapids where Cochinatuck, spirit of the river, dwells.
Just beyond this point, you will find the great sign which you seek...
a red neon one that says 'Willie's Marina'."

Organization chart.

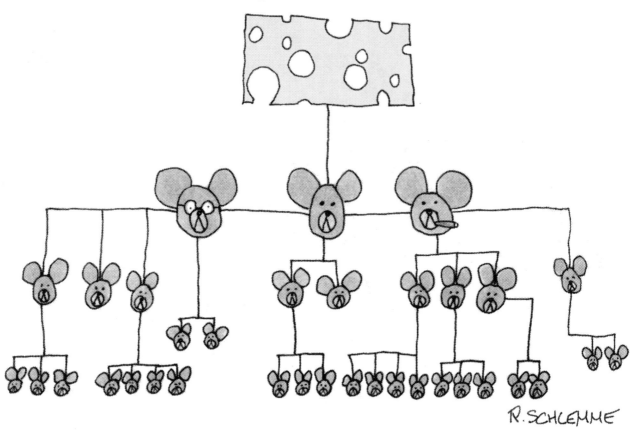

"Rush delivery for Ms. Pandora!
Rush delivery for Ms. Pandora!"

"No, thanks. I'm lactose intolerant."

"I gotta admit, I've never been
awfully keen on *'Realism'*."

In the event you've enjoyed Roy Schlemme's
cartoon takes in *Lightin' Up*, and seek a
little encore, then by all means,
contact **authorhouse.com** immediately
to order one or more of his similar
previously published offerings:
Skewed Views, Skewed Views Too
and/or *The Moon's First Banana.*